I0004220

THE LITTLE BLACK COMPUTER BOOK

JAMES HATCHER

ISBN-13: 978-1496020932
ISBN-10: 1496020936

Available from Amazon.com, CreateSpace.com, and other retail outlets

www.CreateSpace.com/4681848

Printed by CreateSpace, Charleston SC
An Amazon.com Company

IF FOUND, PLEASE RETURN TO:

Name

Address

Phone

Email

Website

Website/Program/Email	Login	Password

Website/Program/Email	Login	Password

Website/Program/Email	Login	Password

Website/Program/Email	Login	Password

Website/Program/Email	Login	Password

Website/Program/Email	Login	Password

Website/Program/Email	Login	Password

Website/Program/Email	Login	Password

Website/Program/Email	Login	Password

Website/Program/Email	Login	Password

Website/Program/Email	Login	Password

Website/Program/Email	Login	Password

Website/Program/Email	Login	Password

Website/Program/Email	Login	Password

Website/Program/Email	Login	Password

Website/Program/Email	Login	Password

Website/Program/Email	Login	Password

Website/Program/Email	Login	Password

Website/Program/Email	Login	Password

Website/Program/Email	Login	Password

Website/Program/Email	Login	Password

Website/Program/Email	Login	Password

Website/Program/Email	Login	Password

Website/Program/Email	Login	Password

Website/Program/Email	Login	Password

Website/Program/Email	Login	Password

Website/Program/Email	Login	Password

Website/Program/Email	Login	Password

Website/Program/Email	Login	Password

Website/Program/Email	Login	Password

Website/Program/Email	Login	Password

Website/Program/Email	Login	Password

Website/Program/Email	Login	Password

Website/Program/Email	Login	Password

Website/Program/Email	Login	Password

Website/Program/Email	Login	Password

Website/Program/Email	Login	Password

Website/Program/Email	Login	Password

Website/Program/Email	Login	Password

Website/Program/Email	Login	Password

Website/Program/Email	Login	Password

Website/Program/Email	Login	Password

Website/Program/Email	Login	Password

Website/Program/Email	Login	Password

Website/Program/Email	Login	Password

Website/Program/Email	Login	Password

Website/Program/Email	Login	Password

Website/Program/Email	Login	Password

Website/Program/Email	Login	Password

Website/Program/Email	Login	Password

Website/Program/Email	Login	Password

Website/Program/Email	Login	Password

Website/Program/Email	Login	Password

Website/Program/Email	Login	Password

Website/Program/Email	Login	Password

Website/Program/Email	Login	Password

Website/Program/Email	Login	Password

Website/Program/Email	Login	Password

Website/Program/Email	Login	Password

Website/Program/Email	Login	Password

Website/Program/Email	Login	Password

Website/Program/Email	Login	Password

Website/Program/Email	Login	Password

Website/Program/Email	Login	Password

Website/Program/Email	Login	Password

Website/Program/Email	Login	Password

Website/Program/Email	Login	Password

Website/Program/Email	Login	Password

Website/Program/Email	Login	Password

Website/Program/Email	Login	Password

Website/Program/Email	Login	Password

Website/Program/Email	Login	Password

Website/Program/Email	Login	Password

Website/Program/Email	Login	Password

Website/Program/Email	Login	Password

Website/Program/Email	Login	Password

Website/Program/Email	Login	Password

Website/Program/Email	Login	Password

Website/Program/Email	Login	Password

Website/Program/Email	Login	Password

Website/Program/Email	Login	Password

Website/Program/Email	Login	Password

Website/Program/Email	Login	Password

Website/Program/Email	Login	Password

Website/Program/Email	Login	Password

Website/Program/Email	Login	Password

Website/Program/Email	Login	Password

Website/Program/Email	Login	Password

Website/Program/Email	Login	Password

Website/Program/Email	Login	Password

Website/Program/Email	Login	Password

Website/Program/Email	Login	Password

Website/Program/Email	Login	Password

Website/Program/Email	Login	Password

Website/Program/Email	Login	Password

Website/Program/Email	Login	Password

Website/Program/Email	Login	Password

Website/Program/Email	Login	Password

Website/Program/Email	Login	Password

Website/Program/Email	Login	Password

www.ingramcontent.com/pod-product-compliance
Lightning Source LLC
Chambersburg PA
CBHW060943050326
40689CB00012B/2558